Making Graphs

Tally Charts

by Vijaya Khisty Bodach

Capstone press

Mankato, Minnesota

A+ Books are published by Capstone Press,
151 Good Counsel Drive, P.O. Box 669, Mankato, Minnesota 56002.
www.capstonepress.com

1 2 3 4 5 6 12 11 10 09 08 07

Library of Congress Cataloging-in-Publication Data
Bodach, Vijaya.
  Tally charts / by Vijaya Khisty Bodach.
    p. cm. —(A+ books. Making graphs)
  Includes bibliographical references and index.
  ISBN-13: 978-1-4296-0043-9 (hardcover)
  ISBN-10: 1-4296-0043-8 (hardcover)
  1. Mathematics—Graphic methods—Juvenile literature. 2. Mathematics—Charts,
diagrams, etc.—Juvenile literature. I. Title. II. Series.
  QA40.5.B642 2008
  510—dc22   2007010814

Summary: Uses simple text and photographs to describe making and using pie graphs.

Editorial Credits
Heather Adamson, editor; Juliette Peters, designer; Wanda Winch, photo researcher;
    Kelly Garvin, photo stylist

Photo Credits
All photos Capstone Press/Karon Dubke, except page 20 Shutterstock/oksanaperkins, page 28
    iStockphoto, and page 29 Shutterstock/Raymond Kasprzak

Capstone Press thanks The Carousel at the Park at Mall of America, Minnesota.

Note to Parents, Teachers, and Librarians
Making Graphs uses color photographs and a nonfiction format to introduce readers to graphing
concepts. *Tally Charts* is designed to be read aloud to a pre-reader, or to be read independently
by an early reader. Images and activities encourage mathematical thinking in early readers
and listeners. The book encourages further learning by including the following sections: Table
of Contents, Glossary, Read More, Internet Sites, and Index. Early readers may need assistance
using these features.

Table of Contents

Try to pick up a stick without moving the pile. How many sticks will each player pick?

We can use tally marks to keep score.
Write the name of each player on a paper.

Line up their sticks next to their names.
Sam picks two sticks before wiggling
the pile. Put his sticks in a row by his name.

Kim grabs five sticks. Tally marks
are made in groups of five. The fifth tally
mark goes across the other four.

Sam's turn again. He picks two more sticks.
Kim takes three sticks on her turn.

Kim is the winner this time.
She scored the most points.

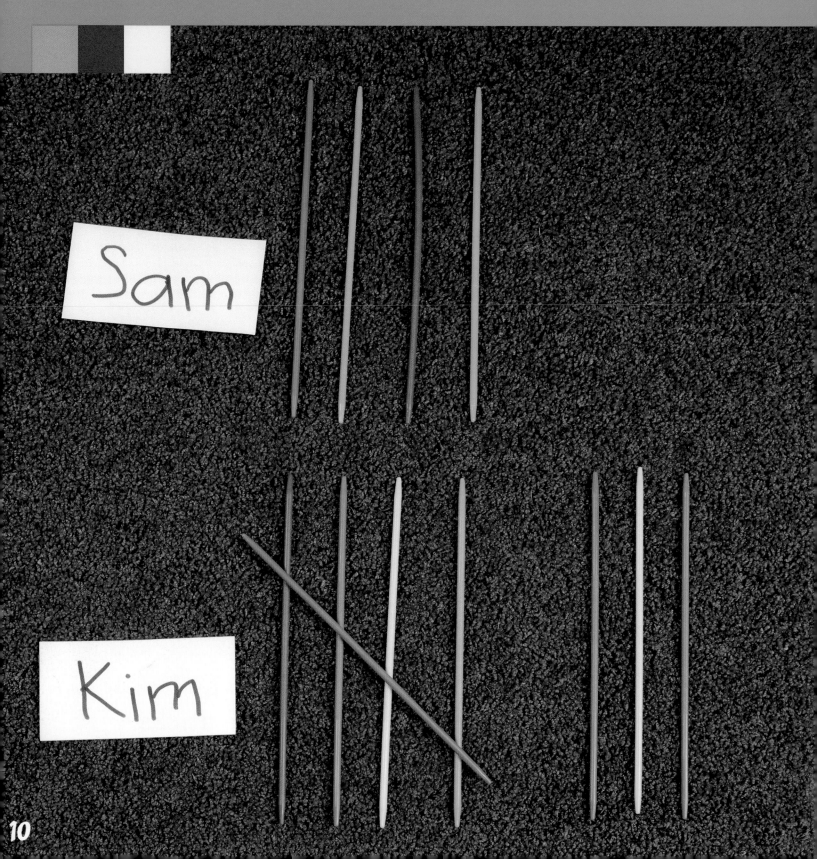

We can keep a tally on paper too.
Tallies help us count things as they happen.

Tally marks help track favorites.
Which flavor of ice cream do people like best?

Vanilla	|
Chocolate	|/|
Strawberry	||

More people like strawberry than vanilla.
But chocolate is the favorite.

What color toothbrush is most popular?
Make a mark for each brush.

Green |\\|

Pink |

Orange ||

Green had the most marks.
It's more popular than orange or pink.

These kids want to play their favorite sports.
Let's take a vote to decide what to play first.

Basketball has the most votes. More kids
want to play basketball than the other sports.

You can use tallies to count cars on a trip.

Write a list of colors.

Mark a line each time a car passes.

Red /

Green

Blue //

A red car goes by. Make a tally mark next to the word red. Next, two blue cars pass.

Red |

Green

Blue ||

A couple more red cars zoom on by.
Then two green cars. And three more blue
cars. Keep making tallies for each car.

Count the tallies and write the totals.
We saw more blue cars than red.
We saw the fewest green cars.

Red ||| ③

Green || ②

Blue   ⅢⅡ   ⑤

We can tally how many free throw baskets each child makes.

Karl made three baskets. Julie made five
baskets. Max had the most free throws.
He made six baskets!

How many coins will land heads up?
Tally marks can help us keep track.

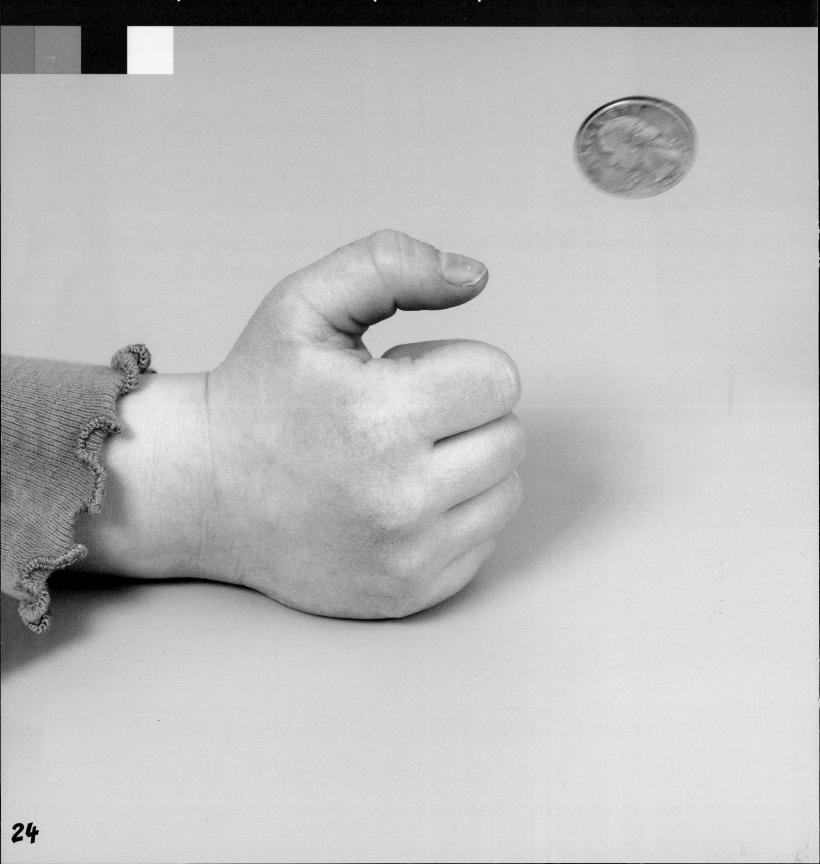

Seven coins landed heads up.

Heads |||| ||

Tails |||

Let's see how many times the carousel spins each ride. Make a tally mark each time the white horse passes.

White Horse

|||| |||| ||

How many tally marks did we make?

A busy bird feeder is fun to watch.
You can use tallies to keep track of the birds.
What type of birds visit each day?
When do more birds visit—morning or evening?

Glossary

carousel (kayr-uh-SELL)—an amusement ride that turns in circles

chart (CHART)—to show information in the form of a picture or graph

favorite (FAY-vuh-rit)—a thing or person that you like best

tally (TAL-ee)—a score or record; a tally mark is one straight line; tallies is the plural of tally.

total (TOH-tuhl)—a number gotten by adding up the whole amount

vote (VOHT)—to make a choice

Read More

Murphy, Stuart J. *Tally O'Malley.* New York: Harper Collins, 2004.

Trumbauer, Lisa. *Let's Graph.* Math. Mankato, Minn.: Yellow Umbrella Books, 2004.

Internet Sites

FactHound offers a safe, fun way to find Internet sites related to this book. All of the sites on FactHound have been researched by our staff.

Here's how:

1. Visit *www.facthound.com*

2. Choose your grade level.

3. Type in this book ID 1429600438 for age-appropriate sites. You may also browse subjects by clicking on letters, or by clicking on pictures and words.

4. Click on the **Fetch It** button.

FactHound will fetch the best sites for you!

Index